# VOICE for LIFE

## SINGER'S WORKBOOK 1: WHITE LEVEL

## CONTENTS



This book belongs to

________________________________

of

______________________________ choir.

# VOICE *for* LIFE

Project editor: Tim Ruffer
Written and edited by Anthony Marks

The White Level of *Voice for Life* was developed by Esther Jones and Leah Perona-Wright in consultation with experienced practitioners from across the UK and beyond. These include: Gordon Appleton, Roger Brice, Lesley Cooper, June Cox, Paul Ellis, Peter Futcher, Susan Gardner, Sally Leeming, Sue Moore, David Ogden, Keith Roberts, Sheila Robertson & Ben Saunders. We are grateful for their contributions.

Design and layout by Anthony Marks

Music origination by Tim Ruffer and Anthony Marks

Illustrations by Hilary Perona-Wright



Printed in Great Britain by Halstan & Co, Amersham, UK

ISBN 978-0-85402-193-2

THE ROYAL SCHOOL OF CHURCH MUSIC
19 The Close, Salisbury, Wiltshire, SP1 2EB
Tel: +44 (0)1722 424848 Fax: +44 (0)1722 424849
E-mail: education@rscm.com Website: www.rscm.com
Registered charity no. 312828

Distributed exclusively in North America by GIA Publications, Inc.
7404 S. Mason Ave., Chicago, IL 60638
Toll free: 800 442 1358 Website: www.giamusic.com

Welcome to *Voice for Life*. We've designed it to help you learn about your voice and develop as a singer. It will encourage you to learn about music and to look at what it means to sing and be a member of a choir.

This White level workbook will help you to practise singing and think about music at home. You will also need to work with your choir trainer, who will explain each new topic and show you what to work on next. Don't try to finish the whole book on your own in a week! You choir trainer will want to be sure you understand each topic fully before you move on to the next stage.

To make the most of your voice you need to practise regularly. This workbook contains breathing and singing exercises to use at home. If you practise on your own as well as with your choir, your singing will quickly improve. As a singer your whole body is your musical instrument. You take it to bed, on the bus, in the car, shopping, to parties and even on holiday. It's important to take care of it all the time. There are tips on how to do this throughout the book.

This workbook contains puzzles and exercises to complete in your own time. But being in a choir is different from being a solo singer because you are also a member of a team. You will have to talk to other members of your choir to find out the answers to some of the questions in this book. Don't worry about doing this – other choir members expect to be asked for information or advice. You will learn about being a good team member, and about making the best contribution you can to your choir.

To complete the White level of *Voice for Life* you must achieve the targets listed on pages 33 and 34. Some targets are about your progress during choir rehearsals, services and other events; some are about things you will do in your own time. As you work through them you will improve as a singer and choir member. After you complete each one your choir trainer will sign a box. You can find out what happens when you complete all the targets by looking inside the back cover of this book. If you want to find anything else in this book, the information on pages 35 and 36 will help you.

Enjoy *Voice for Life!*

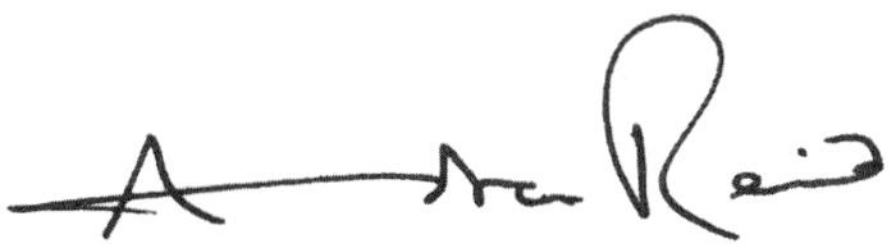

Andrew Reid
Director, RSCM

**Icons** The icons in this book tell you to:

- Read this before going further
- Try a vocal or physical exercise
- Sing something
- Think about something
- Write an answer in the box
- Tick when you have finished an activity

# Thinking about singing

During rehearsal, watch and listen to some of the experienced singers in your choir. (Talk to your choir trainer about this first.) Think about how they look and sound when they sing, then answer the questions below by ticking the boxes.

| | Yes | No | Maybe |
|---|---|---|---|
| Does singing look difficult? | | | |
| Do the singers look relaxed? | | | |
| Does singing sound like hard work? | | | |
| Do they get short of breath? | | | |

Most experienced singers make singing look quite easy. They are relaxed when they sing, and the sound they make is clear and controlled, even if they are singing loudly. They don't seem to be working too hard, and don't get short of breath. This is because they use the whole body when singing, not just the mouth or the throat.

But while it may look easy, singers have a lot to think about – even before they start to think about the music. To sing well, you have to use the whole of your body as a musical instrument. The sound of your voice is affected by many different things, such as:

- how you sit or stand when singing (singers call this **posture**)
- how you control your breathing
- how relaxed or tense you are
- how tired you are
- what you eat and drink

As you progress through *Voice for Life*, you will learn a lot about these different aspects of singing. You will explore many ways of developing your voice, and discover how to use your body to control it.

Starting on the opposite page, there is a basic introduction to the most important aspects of using your voice well. These things need some physical effort and practice, but mainly they require you to concentrate and think carefully about you and your voice.

If some of this seems a bit strange at first, don't worry. Your choir trainer and other members of your choir are there to help you understand how to sing. If you are unsure about what to do, they will be happy to answer questions.

Your posture (how you sit or stand) is one of the most important things about singing. Good posture allows your voice to work at its best. It also gives a good impression to the audience or congregation. Think about posture from the start, as bad habits can be hard to correct later. If your posture is bad, your body can become tense. This makes you tired and affects your singing voice. Here's what you need to know about good posture:

**How to stand when you sing**

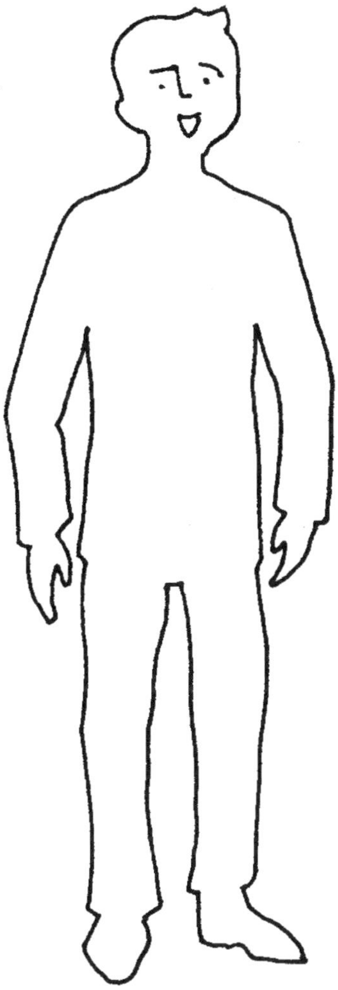

- Stand tall with your head upright
- Relax your shoulders
- Make sure your back is straight but not rigid
- Relax your knees
- Balance your weight evenly on both feet
- Put your feet slightly apart and firmly on the ground

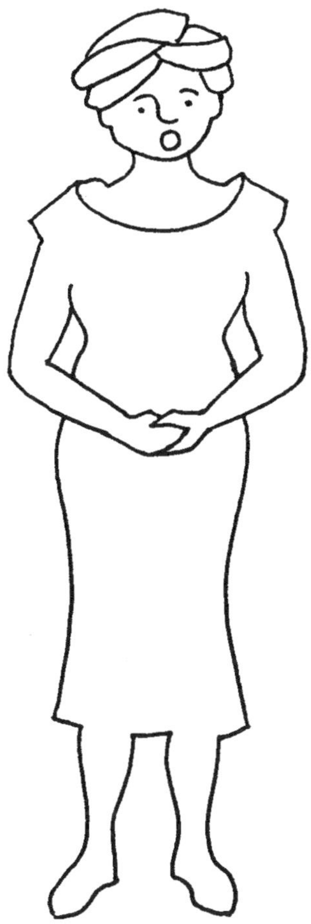

Now try this posture for yourself. It can help to start with your feet, then 'build' your body upwards. Or start with your head, and check everything as you work down to your feet. At first you may feel there's a lot to think about, but with practice it will quickly become more natural.

Sing a few notes, or part of a song. Then take up the standing posture described above. Relax, breathe, and sing the same thing again. Does it feel different? In the box on the right, write some words that describe how this posture feels to you.

**How to sit when you sing**
Usually choirs stand up to sing, but there may be times when you will have to sing sitting down. You can still make a good sound, but you need to be careful about your posture. Here's what you need to know:

- Keep your head and neck upright
- Keep your shoulders relaxed
- Keep your back straight but not rigid
- Keep your feet firmly on the ground

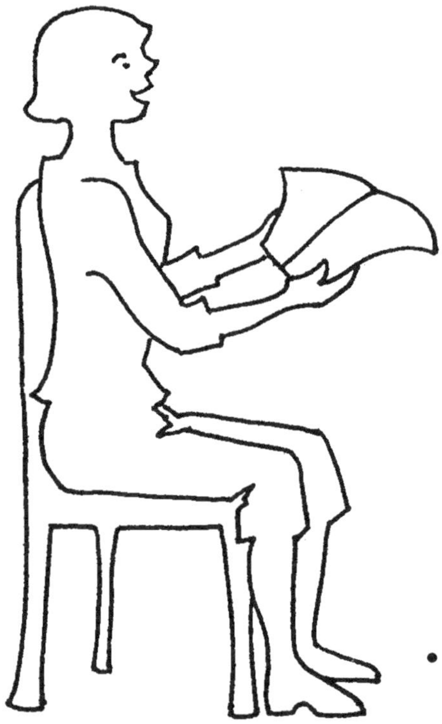

- If your feet don't reach the ground, just sit straight and relaxed

**Posture puzzle**
Put a tick by the singers with good posture.
*Hint: only three of these singers have good posture.*

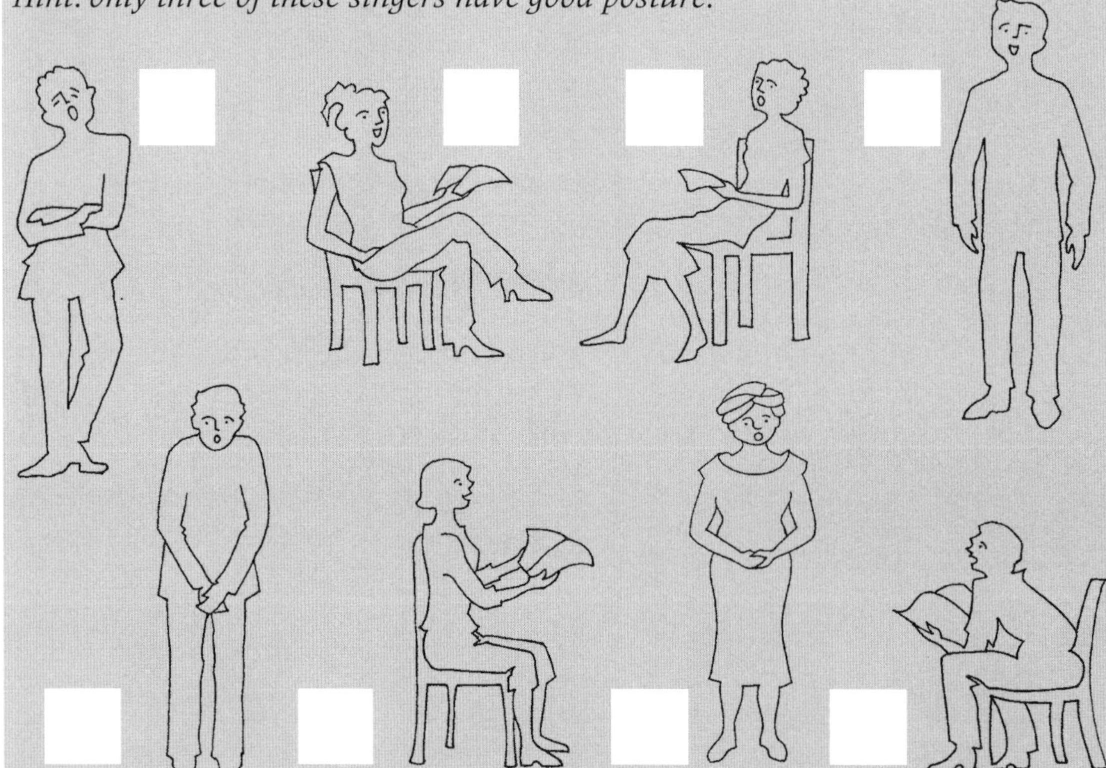

**Holding music**
Choirs often have to hold music books. How you hold your music affects your posture. It also affects whether the audience or congregation can hear your voice, and whether you can see the conductor.

- If you hold your music too high, it blocks your mouth and covers up the sound.

- If you hold your music too low, you have to look down to see it and the sound falls to the floor.

- Hold your music so that you can see the conductor over the top of the music without moving your head.

Look at yourself in a mirror, or ask a friend or your choir trainer to look at your posture. Compare it with the good and bad postures on the opposite page. What is good about the way you stand or sit?

What do you or your choir trainer think you need to work on?

For the White level 'Posture' target (see page 33), you must show you can stand and sit well when singing, holding your music in a good position.

# Breathing

In normal life, you breathe automatically without thinking about it. But when you sing, you need to breathe in a special way and control your breath. Breathing is one of the most important parts of singing. It affects all aspects of your voice – the quality of the sound you make, how long you can sing for, and how comfortable you are when you sing.

For the 'Breathing' target at White level (see page 33), you need to show that you can control your breath well and stay relaxed while you breathe. The exercises here will help you to do this. If you follow the steps below and opposite, and practise them often, your breathing will improve quickly.

The first and most important step to good breathing is to get your posture right. Check your posture whenever you prepare to sing. (If you do this often enough, you will quickly find that you do it without thinking whenever you start singing.) To remind yourself how to stand or sit, look at the good posture pictures on pages 5–7. Then get into a comfortable posture. Relax, and let your body calm down for a while. Ask yourself the questions below:

If you are standing:

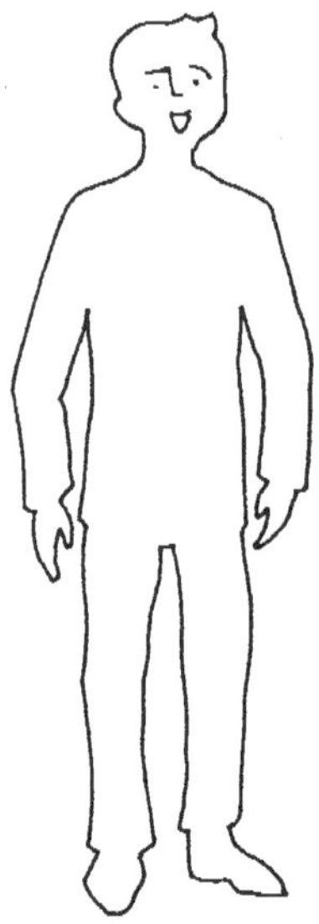

- Am I standing tall?
- Is my head upright?
- Are my shoulders relaxed?
- Is my back straight?
- Are my knees relaxed?
- Is my weight evenly balanced on both feet?

If you are sitting:

- Am I sitting straight?
- Is my head upright?
- Are my shoulders relaxed?
- Is my back straight?
- Are my feet firmly on the ground?

When you can answer 'yes' to all these questions, just stay quiet and alert for a minute or two. Then follow the steps below and opposite:

**1) 'Watch' your breath**
'Watch' your breath without trying to control it. Just let it go in and out automatically. Think about how it feels. Try to relax.

**2) Take some slow, deep breaths**
Next, start to control your breath. Breathe in and out deeply, slowly and gently. Don't gulp air in or force it out. Keep watching yourself as you do this. Feel your chest rise smoothly as you breathe in, and fall as you breathe out. The rest of your body should stay still and relaxed, especially your shoulders.

### 3) Breathe and count

Next, breathe in slowly and count to three in your head. Then hold your breath for another three counts. Finally, count to three again as you breathe out. Do this a few times. Keep your neck and throat relaxed.

| Breathe in | Hold | Breathe out |
|---|---|---|
| Count 1, 2, 3 | Count 1, 2, 3 | Count 1, 2, 3 |

When you can do this comfortably for three counts, try four.

| | | |
|---|---|---|
| Count 1, 2, 3, 4 | Count 1, 2, 3, 4 | Count 1, 2, 3, 4 |

### 4) Breathe and hiss

Repeat step 3, but this time, when you breathe out, make a gentle hiss or say 'shhhh'. Don't force the air out. Keep counting. Stay relaxed.

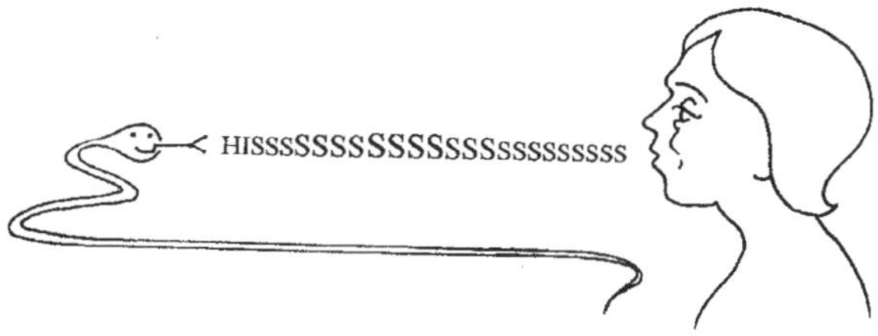


### 5) Breathe and hum

Repeat step 4, but this time, when you breathe out, hum a low, quiet note. Make it as smooth as possible. Later, try this with 'vvv' and 'zzz'.

### Things to think about

When you breathe in, it should be silent. If you hear a noise, it is probably because your throat and neck are tense. Take some deep breaths, relax and try again!

Sometimes, try watching yourself in a mirror as you do these exercises. If your shoulders rise and fall when you breathe, they may be tense. Relax and try again!

### Breathing checklist

After you have practised breathing, tick the boxes when you have:

| | | | |
|---|---|---|---|
| felt your chest rise and fall smoothly | ☐ | checked that your breathing is silent | ☐ |
| felt your breathing become calm and regular | ☐ | checked your shoulders by watching in a mirror | ☐ |
| felt your body relax while you breathe | ☐ | followed steps 1–5 at least 20 times | ☐ |

*VOICE CARE TIP*

*If you feel dizzy, faint or out of breath while singing or practising, stop for a while. Sit down and rest for a few minutes, then start again when you feel better.*

# Voice exercises

Once you have warmed up with breathing exercises, you will be relaxed, alert and ready to exercise your voice. The activities below will help your voice to develop so that singing becomes easier and more enjoyable.

**Voice scribbling**

Move your finger up and down in the air as if you were scribbling, and follow it with your voice. Use a humming sound or 'ooo', and move up and down as high or low as feels comfortable.

Move your finger slowly at first, then speed up. Start quietly, and get louder if you can. You could do this in pairs, singing your partner's scribbles. Remember to stay relaxed.

**Use your voice in different ways**

Making different sounds exercises your voice and loosens it up. Try these:

- Whisper your name

- Quack like a duck
- Say 'Hello' in a sing-song voice

- Bark like a dog

- Imitate a police car siren
- Gasp as if you've just had a shock

**Things to remember**

- Singing is meant to be fun! Stay relaxed, and enjoy your voice and the variety of sounds it can make.
- Your voice may sound quiet at first, but exercise will quickly develop its power.
- Listen to experienced singers in your choir. Also, talk to them about singing.
- Go at your own pace and try not to force your voice to do too much too quickly.

**Where does the voice come from?**
Your voice comes from a part of your throat called the **voice box** or **larynx** (say *'LAR-inks'*). It contains tiny flaps called **vocal folds**. When your breath passes over the vocal folds, they vibrate inside your throat and make the sound of your voice.

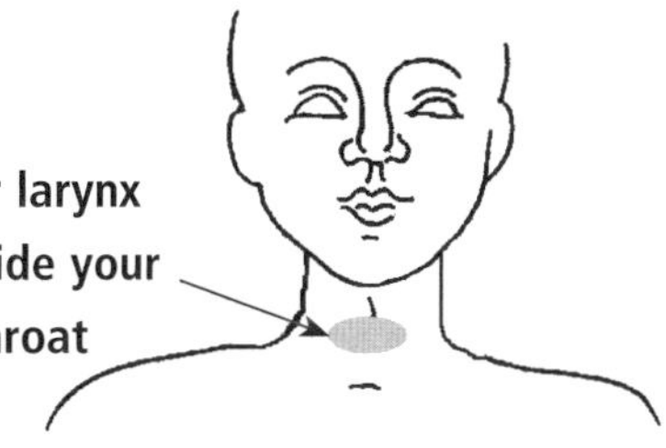


**Feeling your larynx working**
To feel where your larynx is, gently place your hands or fingers on your throat. If you speak or hum, you will feel your larynx vibrate. You can also feel your larynx move upwards when you swallow.

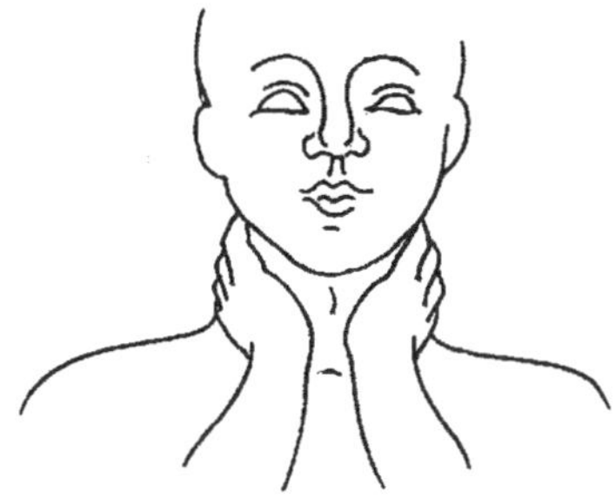

The sound made by your vocal folds alone is very quiet indeed. But the vibrations in your larynx make other parts of your body vibrate too. This makes the sound louder. Singers call this **resonance**.

**Feeling resonance**
You can feel resonance in your face and body. While you hum, gently touch areas of your face such as your jaw, cheeks, nose and forehead. Can you feel the vibrations?

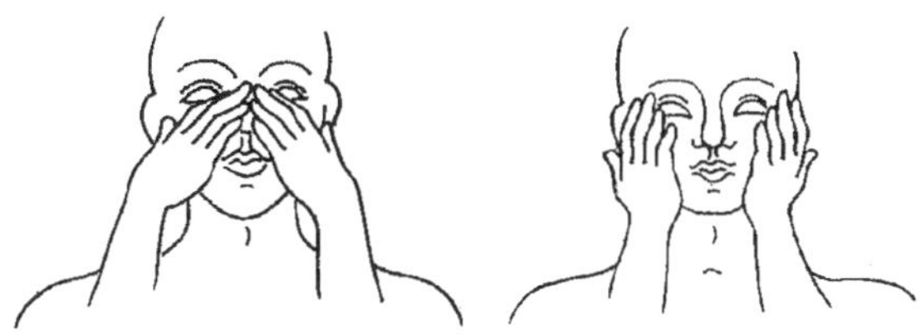

You may need to do this a few times to get used to it. Try touching with your fingertips or the palm of your hand. Don't press hard or you won't feel anything. Next, gently touch your chest and stomach while you are singing, and feel the sound vibrating here too.

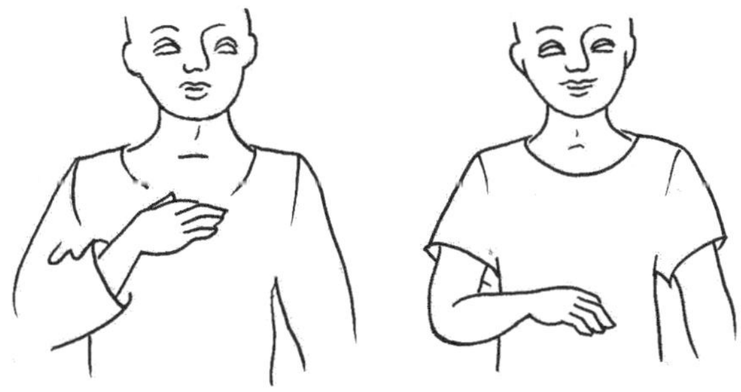

**Voice checklist**

Tick the boxes when you have:

felt your larynx move as you hum, sing or swallow ☐

felt resonance in areas of your face ☐

felt resonance in your chest or stomach ☐

**High and low**

Listen to some other singers, either in your choir or on the radio, a CD or download. Can you hear how some voices sing high notes and some sing low? (Ask your choir trainer about this. He or she may suggest some music to listen to, or find some singers in your choir to help you.)

Singers use the word **pitch** for how high or low a note is. Many things affect the pitch of your voice – whether you are male or female, your age, your size, and your experience as a singer. Usually men sing the lowest pitches in the choir, and women and young people sing the highest.

The distance between the highest pitch you can sing and the lowest is called your **range**. To find your range, first hum a pitch that is comfortably in the middle of your voice.

Then slide up and down as far as you can comfortably go. Never force your voice beyond its range without help from your choir trainer or teacher.

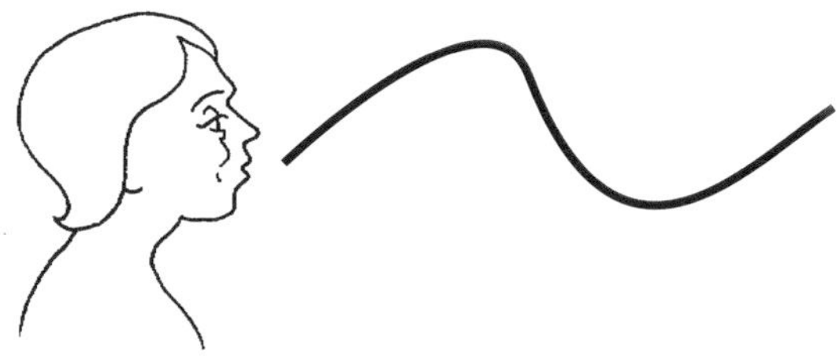

**Voice development**

Your choir trainer will help you find a pitch where your voice feels good, and then develop your range around it. He or she will give you exercises to increase your range and recognize pitches. These will help you with the White level targets for pitch and range (see page 33). Here are some hints and tips to help you focus and strengthen your voice:

- Open your mouth wide when you sing, or the sound will get trapped inside. From time to time, sing in front of a mirror to check your mouth is wide open.

- When you sing, make as much space inside your mouth as you can. Imagine you are biting an apple. Keep your tongue flat and your throat relaxed.

- Exercise your voice regularly and do your practice. Once a week at choir rehearsal probably isn't enough to give you the strength you need.

As a choir member, you have to sing in time and in tune with other singers. The most important things you need to know are:

- when to start and stop singing
- when to take breaths
- what notes and words to sing
- how loudly or quietly to sing
- how quickly or slowly to sing

This is a lot to think about, particularly when you need to control your posture and breathing too. You have two things to help you: the person who conducts or trains your choir, and your music. This page is about working with a conductor or choir trainer, who is responsible for getting the best from your group of singers. The section about music starts on page 14.

**What does a conductor do?**

When you are singing it can be hard to hear other singers, so you may not be able to tell if you are singing well. This is why you need a conductor or choir trainer – someone who hears all the singers and shapes and controls the sound they make together. It is really important to follow the instructions your conductor gives you.

**What should you do?**

The most important thing to do is watch. In choir, make sure you can see the conductor clearly. Find a good place to sit or stand, and hold your music well (see page 7). If you have to look down at your music, you won't be able to see the conductor's gestures. If you can't see, you can't follow the instructions, so you may get lost or make mistakes.

**What do the gestures mean?**

You will learn this by experience. Conductors have different ways of showing you how to sing. At first, the most important instructions will be when to start and end a piece, and how fast and how loud to sing. Most conductors also 'beat time' to show you the pulse of the music (see pages 18-19).

**Conductor checklist**

Tick the boxes when you have:

- found a position in choir where you can see the conductor without difficulty ☐
- watched the conductor throughout a whole piece ☐

**Things to think about**

- If you can't see the conductor, say so! You (or other singers) may need to change position.
- If you don't understand a gesture or instruction, don't be afraid to ask what it means.

Being able to read music is a vital part of being a choir member. It means you can learn pieces more quickly, practise your choir music on your own at home, and understand your conductor's instructions better. If you can't read music, you have to rely on someone else to teach you what to sing.

You don't have to read music at the start of *Voice for Life*, but as you progress through the levels you will learn how to do it. The next few pages are an introduction and will prepare you for the White level targets on pages 33–34.

**Music basics**

The most important details of music are how high or low the notes are (singers call this **pitch**) and how long or short they are (singers call this **duration**). Sing the first part of 'Three Blind Mice' a few times. Think about the patterns it makes. First, listen to how high or low the notes are in relation to each other:

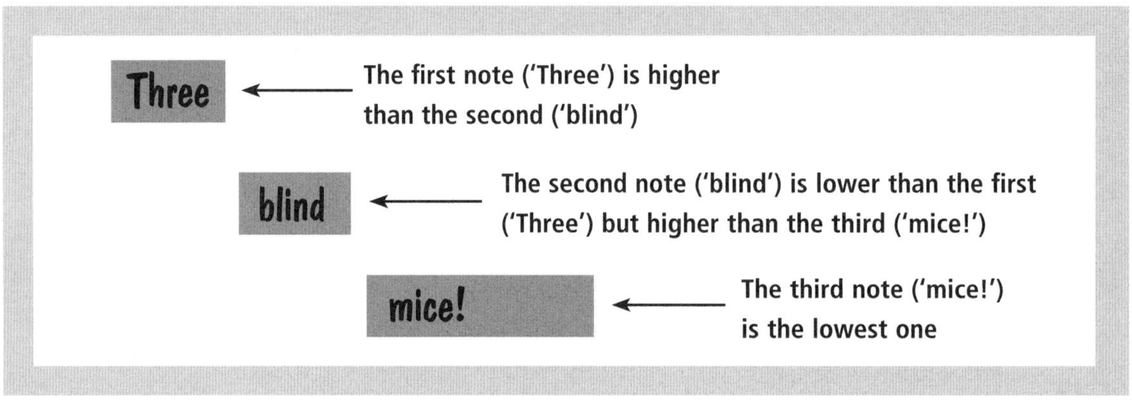


Next, listen to whether the notes are short or long:

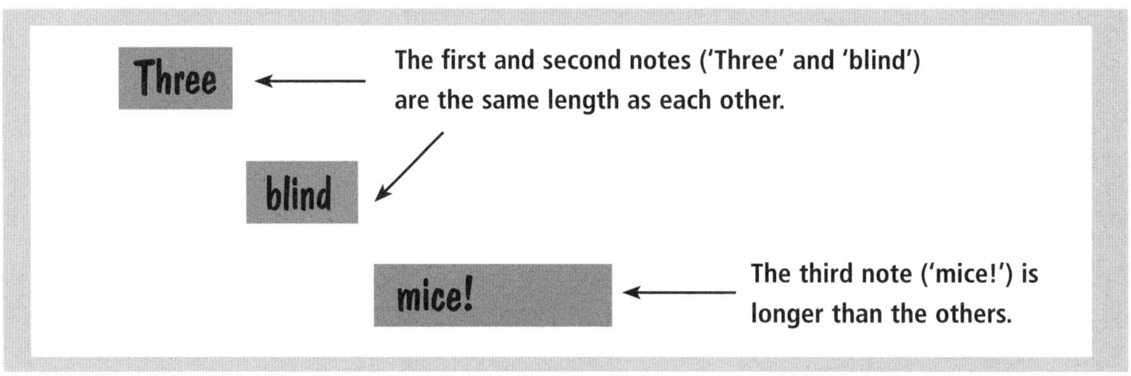


We could write the whole song like this but it would be hard to read, as the words are on different levels. It would take up a lot of space too, as 'See' is higher in pitch than the first three notes, and 'all' is even higher, a jump from the note before it:

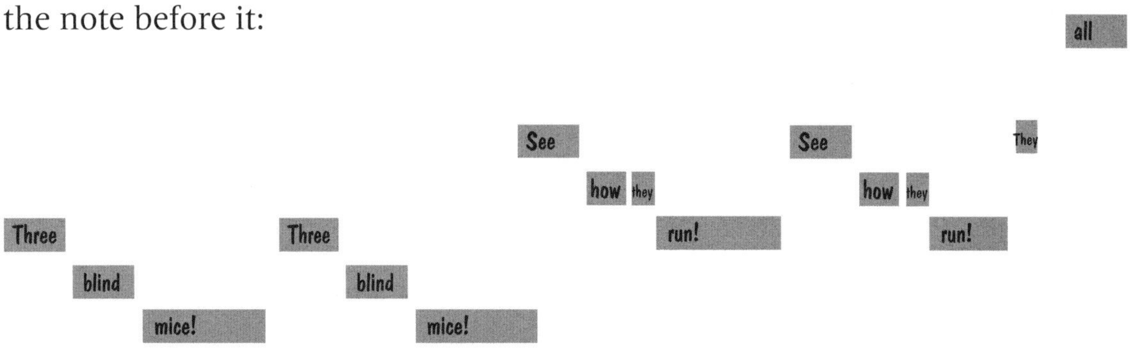

## What music notation tells you

Here is the start of 'Three Blind Mice' in music notation. It takes up much less space than the version opposite, but it still tells you the pitch and duration of the notes, and what words to sing. Sing the first part of 'Three Blind Mice' again and follow the notes and words.

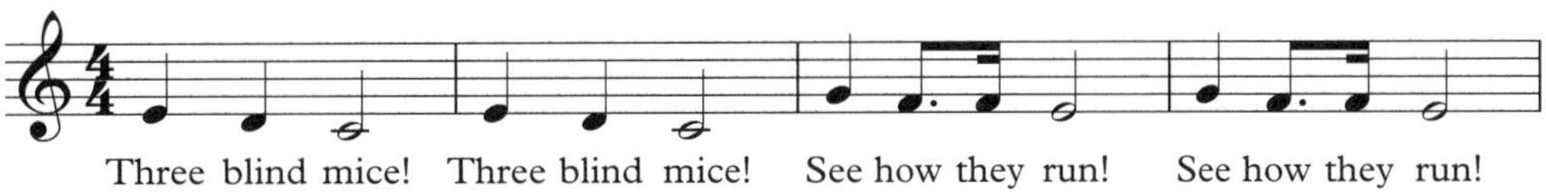


## How music notation works

Music is written on groups of five lines called a **staff** or **stave**.

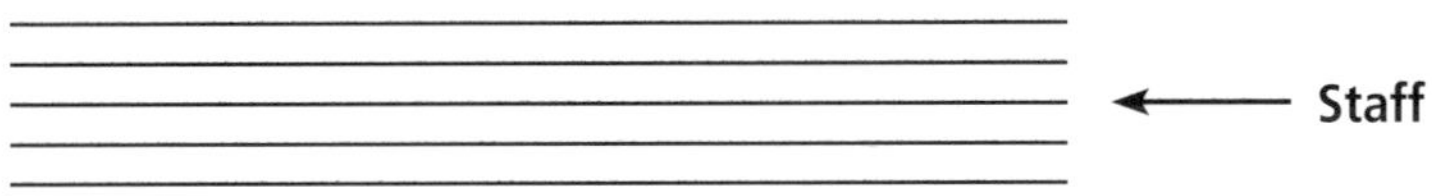


You read the notes from left to right, as you do a book. Notes can be written on the lines:

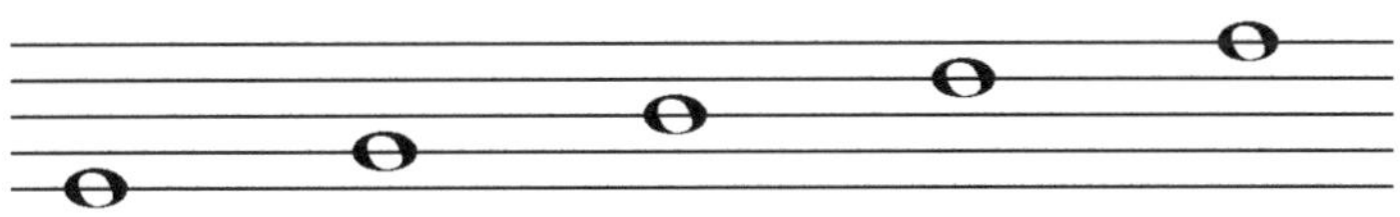

or in the spaces between them.

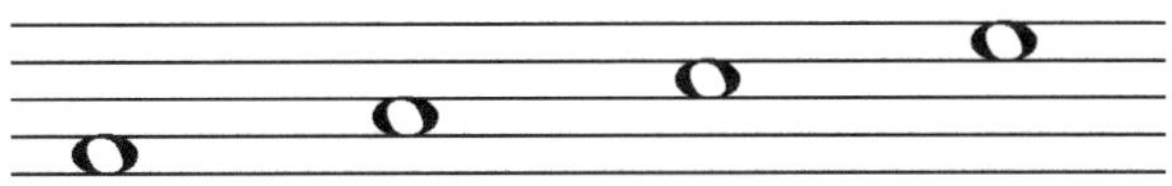

A note at the bottom of the staff is lower in pitch than a note at the top. As you go upwards from one line or space to the next, the notes get higher.

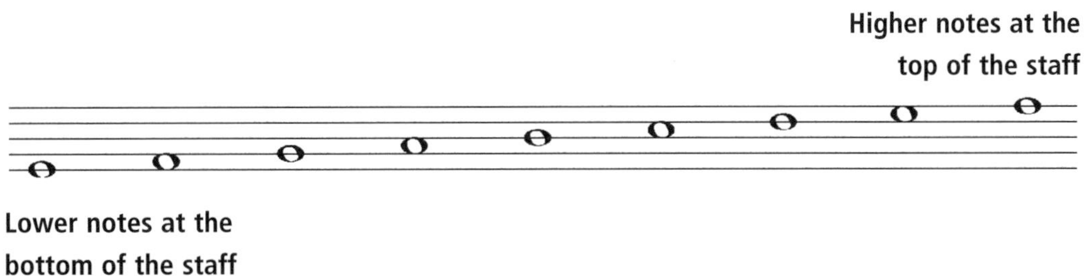


## Pitch puzzle

Draw a ring round the highest note on this staff, and a square round the lowest note.

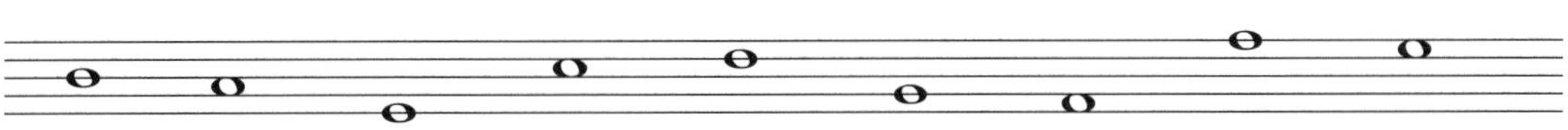

## More about notes

If you look at a piece of printed music, you will see that not all the notes look the same. To describe the differences, you need to know the words for the different parts of a musical note.

- The oval part that sits on the line or in the space is called a **notehead**.
- The stick joined to the notehead is called a **stem.**
- The curved part joined to the end of the stem is called a **tail.**

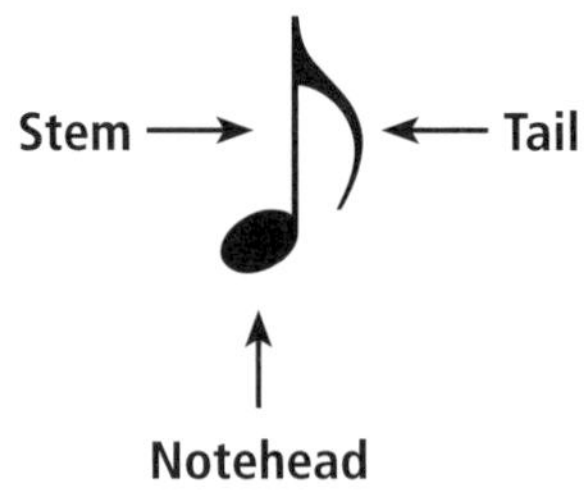


- Notes with tails can be joined together by a longer line called a **beam.**

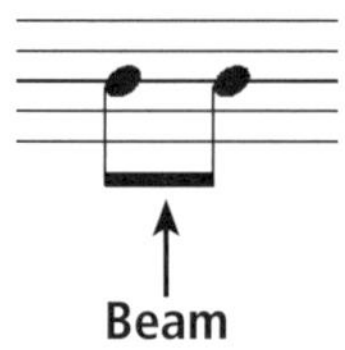


- Stems and tails can point up or down. It doesn't affect the pitch of the note.

## Long and short notes

The position of the notehead on the staff tells you the pitch of the note. Other details tell you about duration.

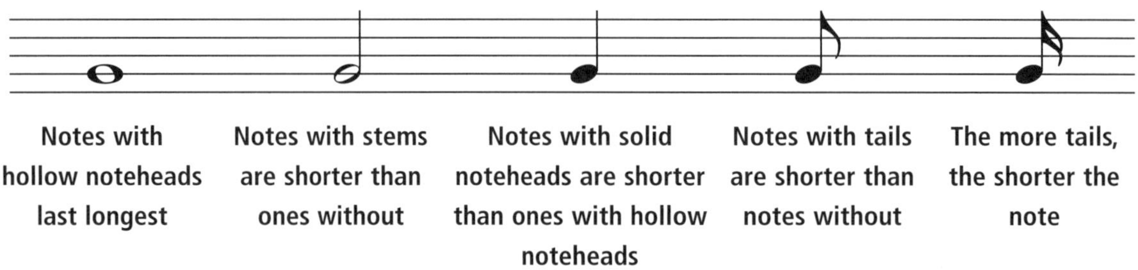


On the staves below, draw some notes like the ones shown above. Make higher and lower notes by putting the noteheads on different lines and spaces on the staff. Make longer and shorter notes by using hollow and solid noteheads, stems and tails.

**More music details**

Think of the lowest and highest pitches you can imagine, or play the lowest and highest notes on a piano or keyboard.

**Lowest pitches at the left-hand end**

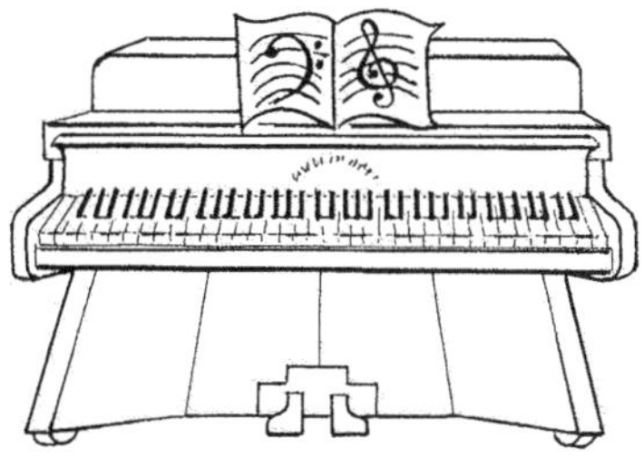

**Highest pitches at the right-hand end**

These pitches are so far apart that you can't write them down on a single five-line staff. Each staff contains a range of pitches, and the range is shown by a special sign at the start of each staff, called a **clef.**

There are two main clefs - the **treble clef** and the **bass clef.**

**Treble clef**

**Bass clef**

A treble clef tells you the music is in a high range. The treble clef is used for high voices (the women or young people in your choir), and high-pitched instruments like violin, flute, or the right hand of the piano.

A bass clef tells you the music is in a low range. The bass clef is used for lower voices (some of the men in your choir), and low-pitched instruments like cello, double bass, or the left hand of the piano.

**High or low?**

Which of these voices or instruments are high, and will use the treble clef? Tick the high ones.

In music, a regular repetition is called a **pulse**. A pulse happens when any sound or movement is repeated regularly. Each individual sound or movement in a pulse is called a **beat**. Here are some examples of pulses in everyday life – can you think of any others?

- Your heartbeat is a pulse.

- The tick of a clock is a pulse.

- A dripping tap is a pulse.

- The flash of a lighthouse is a pulse.

Most music has a pulse. In some styles, it is obvious – you hear it on drums or in handclaps. In other music (choral music for example), you may not hear drums or claps, but the pulse is still there. All the time musicians are feeling, thinking and counting beats in their heads. If there is a conductor, he or she will show the pulse with hand movements or other gestures.

Listen to some music. Try clapping, tapping a finger or moving in time to the pulse. The more you do this, the easier it becomes.

**Long and short notes**
Music is made up of patterns of long and short notes. Written music tells you how long notes last, and how they are grouped together. You 'measure' the length of notes by counting them against beats of the pulse.

**Counting and clapping**
On page 14, we looked at the beginning of 'Three Blind Mice'. We saw how the first and second notes are the same length as each other but the third note is twice as long. To demonstrate this, try this clapping game.

Start by counting 'one, two, three, four' in a regular pattern, over and over. Say 'one' a little bit louder than the other counts. Next, keep counting and start to clap, one clap for each count. Make the first clap in each group of four a little louder than the others. (You could ask a friend to do this with you, as it helps to keep the counting and clapping regular.)

| | | | | | | | | |
|---|---|---|---|---|---|---|---|---|
| COUNT | **one** | two | three | four | **one** | two | three | four |
| CLAP | **X** | x | x | x | **X** | x | x | x |

*VOICE CARE TIP*
*Never chew gum or sweets during a rehearsal or performance.*
*You won't be able to sing at your best, and you could choke.*

When you are comfortable with counting and clapping, stop counting out loud. Instead, sing 'Three Blind Mice' while you clap. Keep the clapping pattern regular. If a friend is helping, both of you can clap, but one of you should count while the other sings. Then answer the questions in the box below.

| | | | | | | | | |
|---|---|---|---|---|---|---|---|---|
| COUNT | one | two | three | four | one | two | three | four |
| CLAP | X | x | x | x | X | x | x | x |
| SING | Three | blind | mice! | | Three | blind | mice! | |

| Three questions about mice | Once | Twice | Three times | Four times |
|---|---|---|---|---|
| How many times do you clap while you sing the word 'Three'? | | | | |
| How many times do you clap while you sing the word 'blind'? | | | | |
| How many times do you clap while you sing the word 'mice'? | | | | |

**Notes in groups**
For 'Three Blind Mice', you clap the pulse in groups of four beats. In music, groups of beats are called **bars.** In written music, bars are separated from each other by vertical lines called **barlines**, so you know when one bar finishes and the next one starts.

The **time signature** tells you how many beats there are in each bar. In 'Three Blind Mice' the time signature is 4/4, which means there are four beats in each bar. Time signatures, barlines and bars (labelled on the music above) help you to count the length of each note and to know where you are in the music.

In the music above, the words 'Three' and 'blind' each last one beat or clap. They are shown by notes with solid noteheads. 'Mice!' is longer. It lasts two beats or claps and is shown by a note with a hollow notehead. (Remember, notes with hollow noteheads always last longer than notes with solid noteheads.) A pattern of long and short notes over a pulse is called a **rhythm.**

# Counting beats and bars

On the staff below you will see a time signature and some barlines. The time signature 4/4 means there are four beats in each bar. If the second number in a time signature is a 4, it means a solid note with a tail lasts for one beat, and a hollow note with a tail lasts for two beats.

Fill up the bars by drawing in some one- and two-beat notes. Make sure each bar contains four beats. The first bar has been done for you.

**Fast, slow and in-between**

The speed of the pulse isn't the same in every piece of music. If the pulse is slow, the music sounds slow because there is more time between each beat and the notes last longer. With a fast pulse, the music sounds more lively because you move more quickly from one beat to the next. In music, the speed of the pulse is called its **tempo**.

Words and symbols on printed music tell the conductor how fast the tempo should be. It's important to watch your conductor, who will indicate the speed of the pulse by hand gestures. The activity below will help you to think about pulse.

**Speed test**

Think of three songs or pieces you like. It's best to use recordings for this because you may need to listen to them a few times, but it could be any music you know well and can sing from memory. You could discuss your choices with your choir trainer.

Listen to each piece. Clap, tap or move in time with the pulse. Which piece has the fastest pulse? Which has the slowest? Which is in the middle? Write the names of your pieces here, fastest at the top and slowest at the bottom.

**... has the fastest pulse**

**... is in the middle**

**... has the slowest pulse**

*VOICE CARE TIP*

*Singing should not hurt your throat. If your throat feels sore when you sing, stop and have a rest. Have a sip of water. If the problem persists, ask your choir trainer for advice.*

4/4 is the most common time signature. In fact it is also known as **common time**. Common time is shown by the symbol on the right, so when you see it at the start of a stave, you know your music has four beats in a bar.

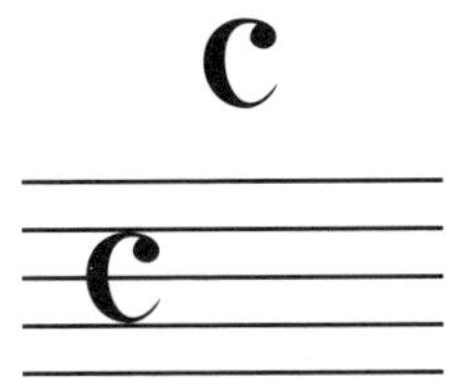

But beats can be collected into groups of other sizes too. Looking at the music below, sing the first few bars of 'Lavender's Blue.' The time signature is 3/4, which means that you count and clap in groups of three, not four.

Clap and count again, this time in groups of three. Make the first beat slightly louder than the other two. When you can do this comfortably, sing 'Lavender's Blue' to this pulse. Do this a few times.

| | | | | | | |
|---|---|---|---|---|---|---|
| COUNT | one | two | three | one | two | three |
| CLAP | X | x | x | X | x | x |
| SING | La - | ven - | der's | blue, | dil - ly | dil - ly |

**Four questions about 3/4**
Look at the music for 'Lavender's Blue' above, then answer the questions about it.

How many bars of music can you see?

Which bar has exactly the same rhythm as the first bar?

How many one-beat notes can you see in the music?

How many notes are joined together by beams?

*VOICE CARE TIP*
*Drink plenty of water before exercising your voice, and while singing. This will make your vocal folds flexible and moist, which is important for keeping your voice healthy.*

# More about counting

**When not to sing**
Notes tell you when to sing, but symbols called **rests** tell you when not to. You don't need to know these in detail for White level, but if you can recognize the most common rests, it makes it easier to count beats in your head and keep your place in the music.

Look at some printed music in a time signature ending in 4. Can you spot any of these symbols?

This rest lasts for one beat

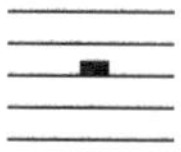

This rest lasts for two beats

This rest lasts for a whole bar

Some rests are short and last a few beats, just long enough for you to take a breath in time for the next notes you have to sing. Other rests can be much longer, especially in a long, complicated piece. When you see rests in your music, count the beats carefully as they go by and watch the conductor, too. If you don't do this, you may not know when you have to start singing again.

**Rest test**
Here are some good and some bad ideas about what to do during rests in the music. Tick the good ones.

☐ Talk to your neighbour

☐ Have a snack

Check your posture ☐

Watch the conductor ☐

Check your phone ☐

Breathe evenly ☐

Have a rest ☐

As a choir member, you need to know what to sing and when to sing it. Your printed music tells you this. For the White level targets (see pages 33–34), you don't have to read music fluently, but you must be able to find your way around it and understand what it tells you.

**Beyond the staff**

Usually you will sing from printed music called a **score**. A score contains the music for all the voices and instruments taking part in the piece. The music for each one is on a separate staff, so that you can see what everyone has to sing or play to make the music complete.

A score is normally made up of several staves, grouped into **systems**. All the staves in a system are linked by a barline running down the left-hand side of the music.

Here is the start of a system of music. In this example there are six staves: four for the voices and two for the organ, bracketed together at the bottom. (Not all music has six staves to each system. It depends how many voices and instruments are taking part.)

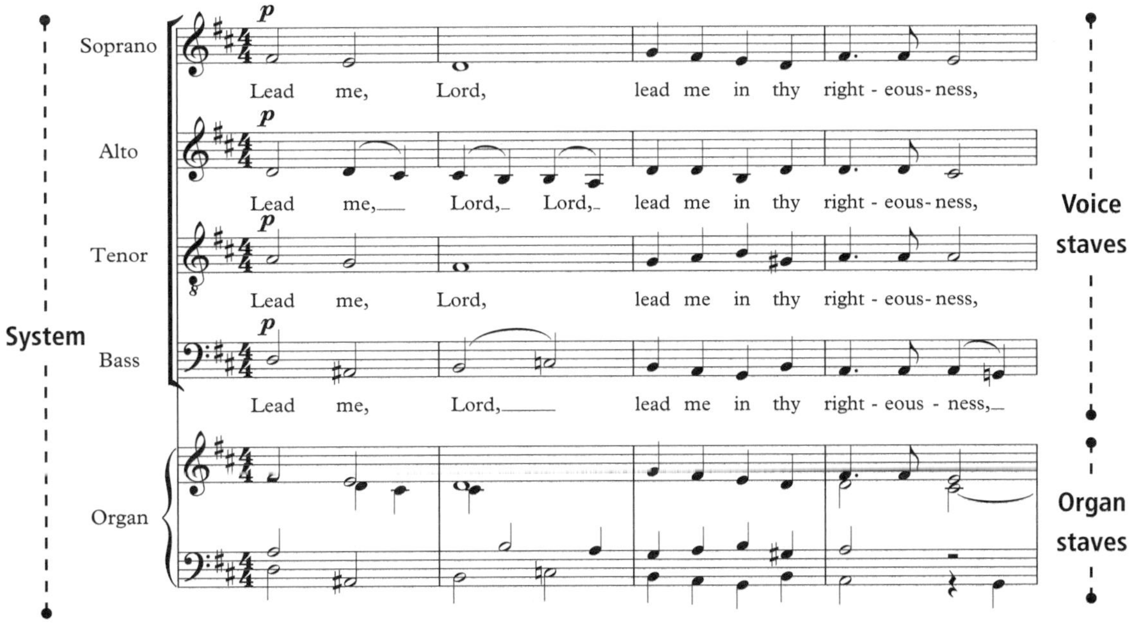


**Symbol search**

In the music above, look for some of the signs and symbols you have already learned earlier in the book. Put a tick in the box when you have spotted them, and circle an example of each on the music.

| | | | |
|---|---|---|---|
| treble clef | ☐ | two-beat note | ☐ |
| bass clef | ☐ | barline | ☐ |
| one-beat note | ☐ | time signature | ☐ |

When singing from a score, you need to know which staff to follow. Normally, singers in choirs are divided into four main groups (called **parts**), depending on how high or low they sing. The parts are called **soprano**, **alto**, **tenor** and **bass**. (Boys and girls who sing the soprano line are sometimes called **trebles.**)

In a score, the voice parts are often written on separate staves, from highest voice to lowest. So the soprano part appears on the top staff, the altos on the second staff down, and so on. If there are instruments in the piece, their parts will appear below the voices. A score with separate staves for all the voices and instruments is called an **open score**.

Let's look in detail at the voice parts in a score.

**Soprano is the highest part. It is sung by women, boys or girls.**

**Alto, the second highest part, can be sung by women or men.**

**Tenor is lower than alto. It is usually sung by men.**

**Bass is the lowest part. It is sung by men with low voices.**

Do you know which part you sing? Circle its name on the music above. If you don't know, don't worry. Ask your conductor or choir trainer to help you with this, and look at the opposite page too.

## Closed scores

A **closed score** has two voice parts on each staff. Sopranos and altos share the top staff: the sopranos sing the notes with stems pointing up. The altos sing those with stems pointing down. Tenors and basses share the bottom staff: tenors sing the notes with stems pointing up and basses those with stems pointing down. Closed score notation is often used for traditional hymns.

**Sopranos and altos share this staff**

**Tenors and basses share this staff**

Circle the name of the part you sing on the music above.

## Knowing which part to sing

Your conductor will tell you which part to sing, depending on the range of your voice. In choir you will stand or sit near others singing the same part.

In a score or a hymn, the staves of the different voice parts are usually labelled on the first system of music (this may just be the initials of the parts: **S A T B**). If for example your conductor asks you to sing alto, find the staff of the alto part on the first system (usually the second one down).

Read your part along the staff from left to right. At the end of the first staff, don't move down to the one below it, as that is sung by the tenors. Instead, jump down to the second staff of the second system and sing that.

Follow the alto line (shown on a grey background) on the score below.

**— — — — — — — Read your part from left to right along the staff — — — — →**

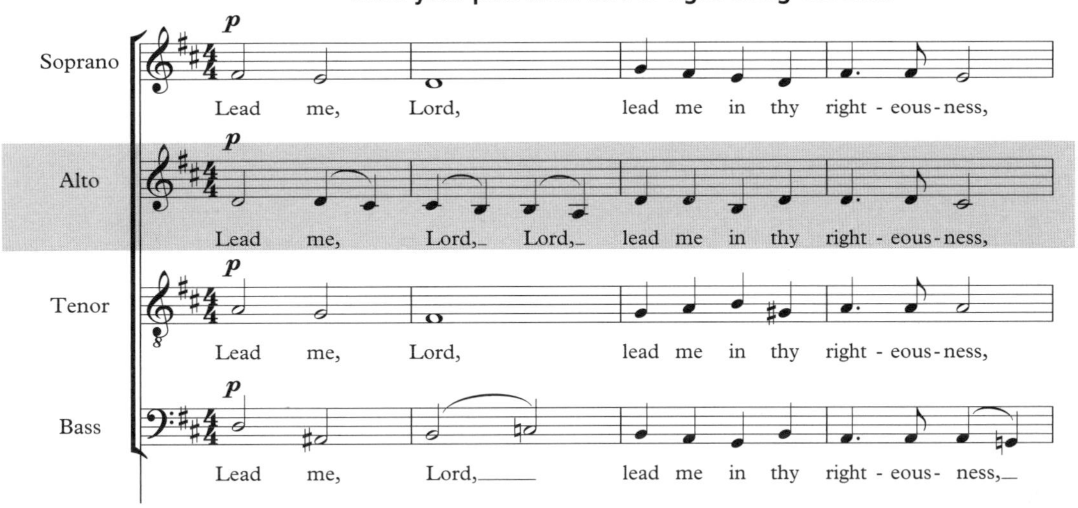


**— — — — — — — Then jump to the same staff in the next system — — — — →**

In the music above, follow each voice part with your finger. When you reach the end of the first staff, jump to the correct staff for that part on the next system. When you have followed each part, tick the box on the right.

| | | | |
|---|---|---|---|
| soprano | ☐ | tenor | ☐ |
| alto | ☐ | bass | ☐ |

# Looking at scores

The more you look at music, the easier it will be to understand and navigate. At first it may seem as though there is a lot to remember, but with practice you will quickly get used to it. The activities on this page will help you to feel more comfortable.

**Score study**
In this activity, you need to look at some pieces of choir music. Ask your conductor or choir trainer to show you some suitable scores. For each piece you look at, answer the questions and fill in the boxes below. (Take photocopies of this page so that you have a sheet to fill in for each piece.)

Write the name of the piece here

How many voice parts are there?

How many instrument parts are there?

Is the piece in open score or closed score (hymn notation)?

What is the time signature of the piece?

Tick when you have:

- followed the part you sing all the way through the piece ☐
- read the words all the way through the piece ☐
- followed another part all the way through the piece ☐

Tick when you have spotted:

| | | |
|---|---|---|
| some one-beat notes ☐ | some one-beat rests ☐ | notes joined by beams ☐ |
| some two-beat notes ☐ | some two-beat rests ☐ | a time signature ☐ |
| some barlines ☐ | a treble clef ☐ | a bass clef ☐ |

**Other ways of finding your way around**

For the White level targets you need to show you can find your place in the piece you are singing. Most music has clues to help you. For example a **double barline** (two thin lines) marks the end of a section in a piece. A **final barline** (one thin line and one thick) usually marks the end of the music.

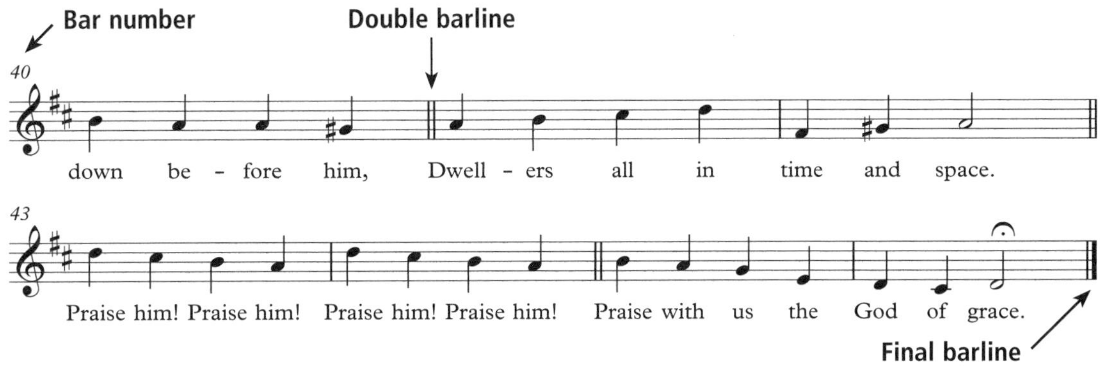


**Bar numbers** help you find where you are in the music without having to count from the start of the piece. You normally find them at the start of each staff or system. They are useful because conductors often want the choir to practise small sections of a piece rather than singing it all the way through.

In the example above, the number 40 means that the bar containing the words 'down before him' is bar 40 of the song. Imagine your conductor tells you to start singing at bar 45: circle your starting note on the music above.

**Upbeats**

Sometimes your conductor may want you to start singing on the last beat of a bar, not the first. The last beat is called an **upbeat**. So 'Start on the upbeat to bar 14' means you start on the last beat of bar 13.

Below is a tune that starts on an upbeat. Imagine your conductor tells you to start singing on the upbeat to bar 4: circle your starting note.

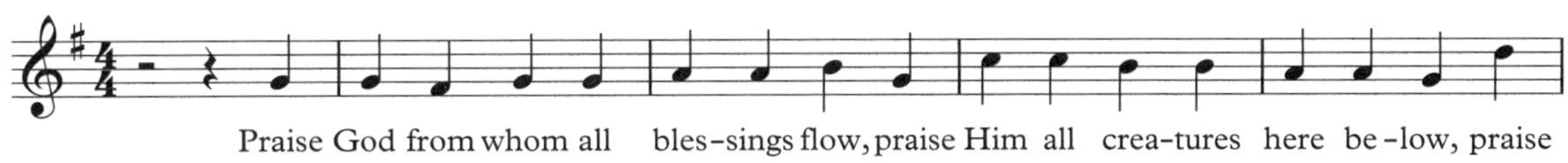


**Bar number volleyball**

Play this with another choir member. You both need a copy of the same piece of music. See how long you can keep going!

1. Player 1 'serves' by shouting out a bar number and the name of a voice part.
2. Player 2 has to find that bar number and part, and say the words in it.
3. If player 2 is correct, he or she shouts out another bar number and voice part for player 1 to find.
4. If one player makes a mistake, the other gets a point and serves again.

# Signs and symbols

Pieces of music don't always go straight through the score from start to finish. Some scores contain symbols called **repeats** that tell you to sing part of the music more than once. Repeats tell you to move around the score. You need to be able to recognize them so that you don't get lost. Remember to watch your conductor, who will help you with this.

The two most common repeat signs are shown on the right. They appear in the music instead of ordinary barlines. You have to sing the music between the repeat signs twice, then continue with the rest of the piece.

**This sign shows where the repeated section starts.**

**And this one shows where it ends.**

In the music below, draw a line under the bars you have to sing twice.

Traditional French carol

**Other kinds of repeat**

Music contains other kinds of symbol to tell you to repeat sections in a score. You don't need to know about these in detail for White level targets. However if you can recognize them, you will know to expect a repeat. Again, it will help if you listen carefully to your conductor's instructions.

***Da Capo*** or ***D. C.*** means 'Go back to the beginning'.

A ***coda*** is a section that comes at the end of a piece of music. Here is a coda sign:

***Dal Segno*** or ***D. S.*** means 'Go back to the sign'. Look for this sign to go back to.

***Fine*** (say *FEE-nay*) means 'the end'. You may see this at the end of a piece, or of a repeated section.

**Understanding repeats**

When your choir starts learning a new piece, your conductor will explain any repeats so you know which parts to sing twice. If anything is unclear, don't worry about asking. Even experienced singers find repeats tricky.

**Symbol search repeated**

Look through some scores and see if you can spot some of the symbols you have learned on this page. Tick when you have spotted:

a 'start repeat' ☐

an 'end repeat' ☐

a *segno* ☐

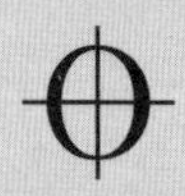

a coda ☐

The instructions ***D.C.*** or ***D.S.*** ☐

***Fine*** at the end of a piece ☐

As well as high, low, long and short, notes can be loud or quiet (this is sometimes called **volume**). Listen to some choir music or remember pieces you have sung, and think about the loud and quiet parts. (Ask your conductor or choir trainer about techniques for singing loudly without straining your voice.)

To tell you how loudly to sing, printed music contains instructions called **dynamics**. They are often written in Italian, because the first music printers were Italian. Sometimes you will see whole words, sometimes just symbols. Here are the most important words and symbols:

| Symbol | Italian word | Pronunciation | Meaning |
|---|---|---|---|
| ***p*** | ***piano*** | *pee-AH-no* | quietly |
| ***f*** | ***forte*** | *FOR-tay* | loudly |
| ***pp*** | ***pianissimo*** | *pee-a-NISS-im-o* | very quietly |
| ***ff*** | ***fortissimo*** | *for-TISS-im-o* | very loudly |

The Italian word *mezzo* (say *met-so*) means 'half' or 'middle'. So:

| | | | |
|---|---|---|---|
| ***mp*** | ***mezzo piano*** | *MET-so pee-AH-no* | fairly quietly |
| ***mf*** | ***mezzo forte*** | *MET-so FOR-tay* | fairly loudly |

Can you put the six symbols above in order of loudness, from quietest to loudest? Some of them have been done for you.

| | | | | | |
|---|---|---|---|---|---|
| ***pp*** | | ***mp*** | | ***f*** | |

You will often see a dynamic sign at the beginning of a piece, followed by a different one later in the piece. This tells you to change volume. Some dynamics tell you to change volume gradually, that is, to get louder or quieter bit by bit.

| Symbol | Italian word | Pronunciation | Meaning |
|---|---|---|---|
| ***cresc.*** or < | ***crescendo*** | *cresh-END-o* | get gradually louder |
| ***dim.*** or > | ***diminuendo*** | *di-min-you-END-o* | get gradually quieter |

Look at some printed music and see if you can spot some of these signs and symbols.

You will now be familiar with many music signs and symbols, but learning to read music fluently takes time. Don't worry if you don't recognize everything immediately. *Voice for Life* will help you develop this skill.

For White level, you don't have to understand everything you see. However on this page you can find out about a few more symbols that will help you as a singer. They are mainly about breathing and how long to hold notes.

This sign is called a **pause** or **fermata.** It tells you to hold a note longer than its normal value. This means you need to watch the conductor even more carefully than usual.

This tick sign is a **breath mark.** It tells you to take a breath before singing the next note. Sometimes a comma is used instead of a tick.

**Marking your own music**

You will often see pauses and breath marks printed in music, but your conductor might want you to pause or take an extra breath that you need to write into your own score. Take a pencil with you to rehearsals in case you are asked to do this. Here are some extra signs that may be useful:

Musicians often draw a little pair of glasses on the music. This is to remind them to watch the conductor if the music is particularly complicated.

The letters V. S. stand for ***volti subito***, which means 'turn the page quickly'. You may see this printed in the score, or you may write it in yourself as a reminder.

**V. S.**

**Sign time**

In the boxes below, draw the signs that tell you to:

| | | | |
|---|---|---|---|
| sing very loudly | | watch the conductor | |
| hold the note longer | | get louder | |
| take a breath (both signs) | | sing fairly quietly | |

# Understanding the music we sing

As a choral singer, you sing for an audience or congregation. To do this well, you must understand the meaning of the words and the mood or background of each piece you learn. Your conductor will help, but you can do a few important things for yourself between rehearsals:

- Read the words of the piece aloud all the way through. Follow the line you sing in the music. Imagine you are telling a story.
- Think about the mood and meaning of the words. (Are they happy or sad? Do they tell a story? Are they connected with a particular event or festival?)
- Make a note of any words you don't understand, or don't know how to pronounce. At your next rehearsal, ask your conductor or another choir member.
- Learn some of the words from memory. This makes rehearsals more enjoyable.

Like a story or a poem, music has to be written or created. Someone who writes music is called a **composer** or **arranger**. For each piece you sing, find out this person's name. (Ask another choir member if you aren't sure.)

**Score study**

For each new piece you start, copy this page and fill in the boxes below.

| |
|---|
| Write the name of the piece here ... |
| ... and the name of the composer or arranger here. |

Tick when you:

| | | | |
|---|---|---|---|
| have read the words from start to finish | ☐ | can say some of the words from memory | ☐ |

| | |
|---|---|
| What is the mood of the piece? | Is it for a particular event or festival? |

| |
|---|
| Make a note of any words you don't understand. |

*You may photocopy this page*

# Singing as part of a choir

As a singer, you need to practise on your own to develop your voice and musical ability. But as a member of a choir, you are part of a team of singers. If the team is to achieve its best, every individual member has to do his or her best, too. Singing in a choir is easier and more enjoyable if all choir members take their responsibilities seriously.

To achieve the White level targets for this module (see page 34) you need to demonstrate that you understand what it means to belong to your choir and what is expected of you. Your conductor and other choir members will help you with this, but here are some things to think about.

**Rehearsals**

Go to rehearsals as often as possible. Singers who miss rehearsals hold up the rest of the choir, as the conductor has to spend time repeating instructions and advice. Here's how to make the most of rehearsals:

- Arrive on time. Make sure you know where to stand or sit.
- Concentrate and watch the conductor.
- Make sure you bring your music to rehearsal, and a pencil to make notes if necessary.
- If you have to miss a rehearsal or performance, warn your conductor as early as possible.
- If you do have to miss a rehearsal, try to find out from another choir member what you missed.

**Performances**

You have a responsibility to everyone else in your choir to try your hardest during performances, concerts or services. This means:

- Arrive on time.
- Make sure you know any special instructions for the performance. (If you are unsure, ask another choir member.)
- Make sure you are relaxed, ready to sing and focused.
- Look after your voice and keep it in good singing condition.

*VOICE CARE TIP*

*Dairy products and some fruit juices cause congestion in the throat. This can make it feel as if you need to swallow a lot, cough, or clear your throat. Try to avoid chocolate, cheese, milk, and other dairy products before you sing. Drink water, not juice.*

The targets for the White level of *Voice for Life* are listed on this page and the next. As you work through this book, you will learn to do all the things below. This section is a record of your progress, so write your name here.

________________________________________

Each time you achieve a target, your choir trainer will sign the box and record the date. There is no time limit to complete the targets. It is more important to learn everything thoroughly than to rush to finish the book. Your choir trainer will make sure that you make steady progress so that when you finish the book you are prepared for the next level.

When all the boxes are signed, you have successfully completed White level. Your choir trainer will sign the declaration inside the back cover of this book, where you can also find out what happens next.

**Module A: Using the voice well**

The singer understands the need for regular practice and is able to:

| | Signed: | Date: |
|---|---|---|
| • stand and sit with good posture while singing, holding music appropriately | | |
| • demonstrate good breath control using the exercises on pages 8 and 9 | | |
| • sing with focus and concentration in rehearsals, performances and services | | |
| • follow the conductor at key moments in a piece (such as the start and end) | | |

**Module B: Musical skills and understanding**

The singer has completed the theory section of the White workbook and is able to:

| | Signed: | Date: |
|---|---|---|
| • match the pitch of a note played on the piano (within an appropriate range) | | |
| • sing five notes that move up and down by step | | |
| • identify which of two notes is higher or lower in pitch | | |

**Module B** *continued*

| | Signed: | Date: |
|---|---|---|
| • sing back a simple one-bar melody with a five-note range | | |
| • clap in time to a familiar song or hymn | | |
| • find his or her place in a musical score using bar numbers | | |
| • understand common music symbols, including repeats, breath marks and pauses | | |
| • identify his or her voice part in a score | | |
| • understand basic dynamic markings (***pp, p, mp, mf, f, ff,*** *crescendo* and *diminuendo*) | | |

**Module C: Repertoire**
The singer has:

| | Signed: | Date: |
|---|---|---|
| • filled in the sheet on page 31 for at least three pieces of music | | |

**Module D: Belonging to the choir**
The singer is a responsible choir member and:

| | Signed: | Date: |
|---|---|---|
| • attends rehearsals regularly and punctually | | |
| • tells the choir director in advance when he or she is going to be absent | | |
| • makes a positive contribution to the choir | | |
| • has met other target(s) as specified by the choir director | | |

On this page you can find many of the signs and symbols you will find in the music you sing. All of them are described in this book. For more detailed explanations, go to the pages listed under each heading.

### The staff or stave (page 15)

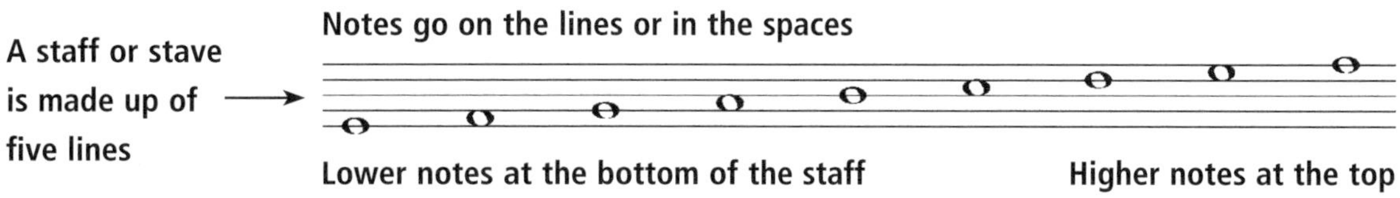


### How notes are built (page 16)

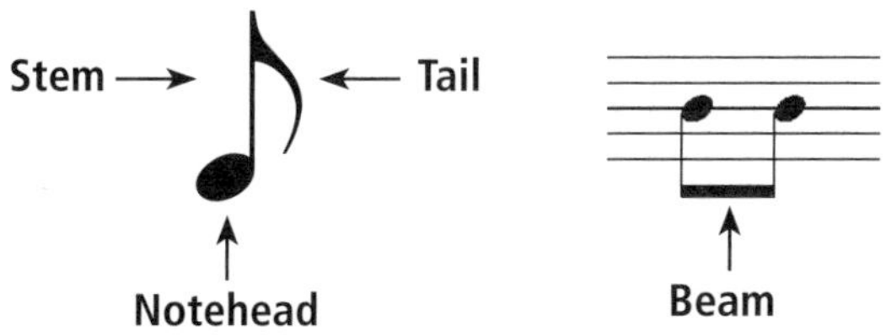


### Clefs (page 17)

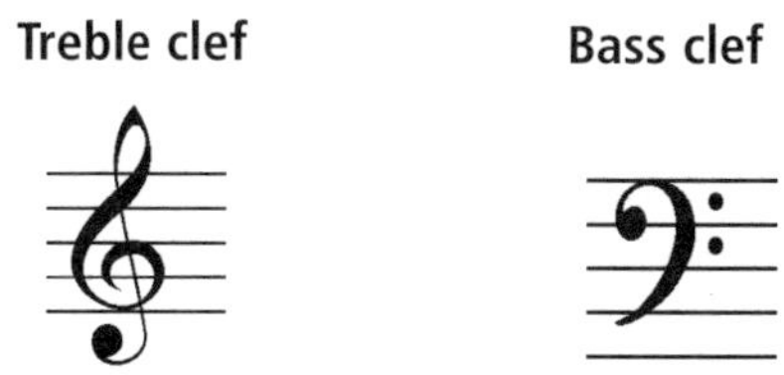


### Notes in groups (page 19)

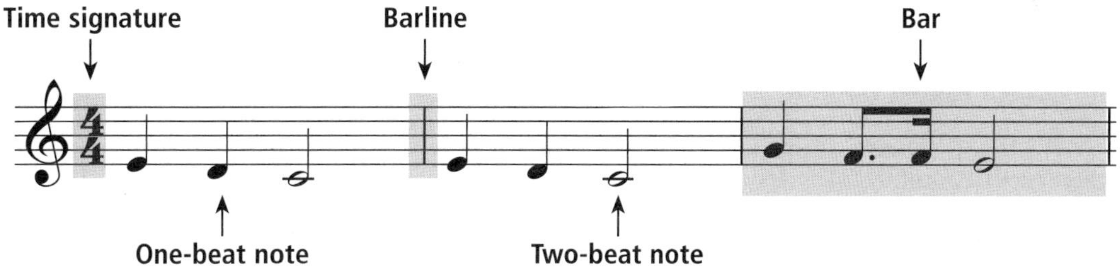


### Time signatures (pages 19 and 21)

### Rests (page 22)

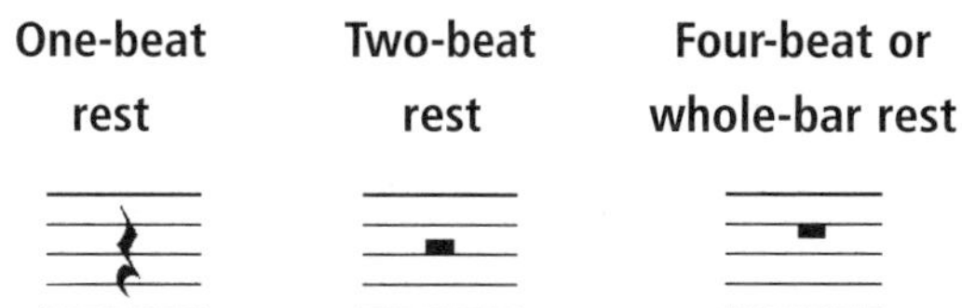


### Barlines and repeats (pages 27 -28)

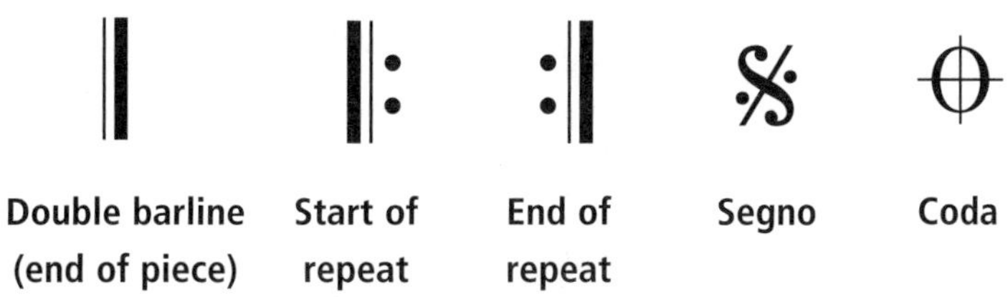


### Dynamics (page 29)

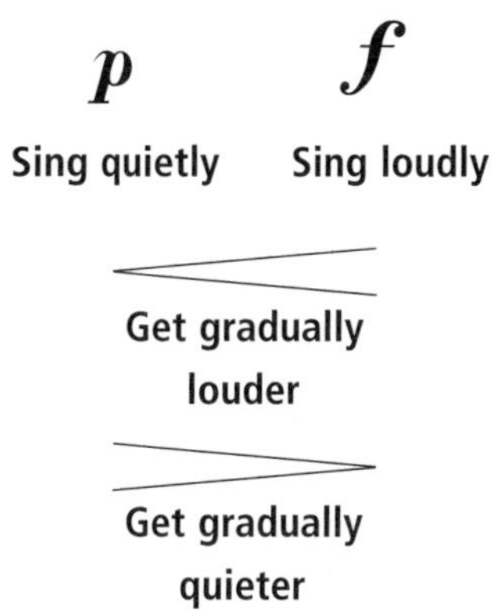


### More signs and symbols (page 30)

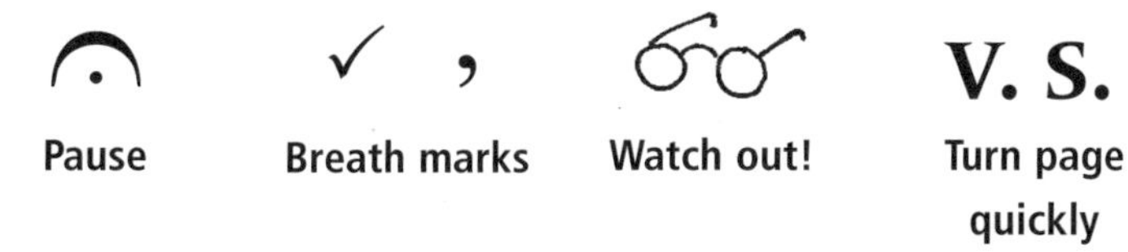

# Index

Important words used in this book are explained briefly here. For more detailed explanations, go to the pages listed under each heading. Any word in **bold type** also has an entry in the index.